Collins

AQA GCSE 9-1
English Language

Target Grade 5 Workbook

Jo Heathcote and Sheila McCann

Acknowledgements

The author and publisher are grateful to the copyright holders for permission to use quoted materials and images.

Extract on page 34 from *Looking for Adventure* by Steve Backshall, Swordfish published by Orion Publishing, The Orion Publishing Group, London

All images © Shutterstock.com

Every effort has been made to trace copyright holders and obtain their permission for the use of copyright material. The author and publisher will gladly receive information enabling them to rectify any error or omission in subsequent editions. All facts are correct at time of going to press.

Published by Collins
An imprint of HarperCollins*Publishers*
1 London Bridge Street
London SE1 9GF

HarperCollins*Publishers*
Macken House, 39/40 Mayor Street Upper,
Dublin 1, D01 C9W8, Ireland

© HarperCollins*Publishers* Limited 2025

ISBN 9780008784584

First published 2025

10 9 8 7 6 5 4 3

All rights reserved. No part of this publication may be reproduced, stored in a retrieval system, or transmitted, in any form or by any means, electronic, mechanical, photocopying, recording or otherwise, without the prior permission of Collins.

Without limiting the exclusive rights of any author, contributor or the publisher of this publication, any unauthorised use of this publication to train generative artificial intelligence (AI) technologies is expressly prohibited. HarperCollins also exercise their rights under Article 4(3) of the Digital Single Market Directive 2019/790 and expressly reserve this publication from the text and data mining exception.

British Library Cataloguing in Publication Data.

A CIP record of this book is available from the British Library.

Commissioning Editors: Kerry Ferguson and Clare Souza
Authors: Jo Heathcote and Sheila McCann
Editors: Charlotte Christensen and Richard Toms
Cover Design: Paul Oates
Inside Text Design and Layout: Ian Wrigley
Production: Bethany Brohm
Printed and bound by Ashford Colour Ltd

MIX
Paper | Supporting responsible forestry
FSC™ C007454

This book contains FSC™ certified paper and other controlled sources to ensure responsible forest management.

For more information visit: www.harpercollins.co.uk/green

Contents

How to Use this Book 4

Paper 1: Explorations in creative reading and writing

Paper 1 Overview 5
Section A: Reading 6
Section B: Writing 16
Responses to Paper 1 21

Paper 2: Writers' viewpoints and perspectives

Paper 2 Overview 33
Section A: Reading 34
Section B: Writing 46
Responses to Paper 2 51

How to Use this Book

This workbook contains all of the source material and exam practice questions for both Paper 1 and Paper 2 of GCSE English Language. The sources and questions have been modelled on the ones you will sit in your AQA GCSE 9–1 English Language exam. Writing space has been included to allow you to write your answers in the book.

There are a couple of ways you can use this workbook.

1. **As a set of mock exams:**

    You could set aside the correct time slot for each paper and complete the examination-style questions under timed conditions. This will help you to experience what it will be like on the day of the real exam. It's a good idea to use the workbook in this way if you are already confident with your skills.

    Once you have completed each exam, there are sample answers and AQA-style mark scheme grids for you to match your own responses against. The relevant level has been shaded in green in the marking grids.

    A good way to check your response is to ask yourself if your own answer seems:
    - stronger than the sample response
    - weaker than the sample response
    - **or** similar to the sample response.

2. **As a step-by-step skills booster and revision programme:**

    Here you might focus on one question at a time. Remind yourself of the skills you think you need for each question. Read the 'Checklist for success' to help you with this. Write your own response.

    Once you have answered a question, carefully check your response against the sample answer, making notes for yourself in the 'My checklist for success' box of any skills you might have missed. Read the 'Commentary' box, which explains how the sample answer has been structured and what effect the writing has.

    In this way you can work at your own pace and spend more time on the questions you are unsure of in order to really boost your skills.

An ebook version of this workbook can be downloaded for free. For access to the ebook, visit **www.collinshub.co.uk/ebooks** and follow the step-by-step instructions.

Paper 1: Explorations in creative reading and writing

Paper 1 Overview

In *Paper 1 Explorations in creative reading and writing* there are two sections: **Section A Reading** and **Section B Writing**. Questions will be based on a source, which will be one single text.

The maximum marks for this paper are 80 marks and the time allowed is 1 hour 45 minutes. You are advised to spend about 15 minutes reading through the source and the five questions that you need to answer before you begin writing. You should also allow enough time at the end to read through / check your answers.

In Paper 1 Section A of the exam, you will be assessed on the quality of your **reading**. You will be asked to read a piece of source material from a short story or novel from the 20th or 21st century. You are unlikely to have seen the passage before.

Your job is to apply your skills of reading and analysis to answer the questions about the passage.

You are advised to spend about **1 hour** on this section. You need to read and complete **four** questions worth **40 marks** – half of the marks for the paper.

In Paper 1 Section B of the exam, you will be assessed on the quality of your **writing**. You will be asked to write an extended writing response to either a descriptive task or a narrative task.

You are advised to spend about **45 minutes** on this section. You need to complete **one** question worth **40 marks** – half of the marks for the paper. You will be awarded up to 24 marks for content and organisation, and up to 16 marks for technical accuracy.

Section A: Reading

Begin by reading carefully the extract below from *The Great Gatsby* by F. Scott Fitzgerald, published in 1925. In it, the narrator Nick Carraway describes the amazing parties held by his very wealthy neighbour, Jay Gatsby.

There was music from my neighbour's house through the summer nights. In his blue gardens men and girls came and went like moths among the whisperings and the champagne and the stars. At high tide in the afternoon I watched his guests diving from the tower of his raft, or taking the sun on the hot sand of his beach while his two motor-boats slit the waters of the Sound, drawing aquaplanes over
5 cataracts of foam. On week-ends his Rolls-Royce became an omnibus, bearing parties to and from the city between nine in the morning and long past midnight, while his station wagon scampered like a brisk yellow bug to meet all trains. And on Mondays eight servants, including an extra gardener, toiled all day with mops and scrubbing-brushes and hammers and garden-shears, repairing the ravages of the night before.

10 Every Friday five crates of oranges and lemons arrived from a fruiterer in New York — every Monday these same oranges and lemons left his back door in a pyramid of pulpless halves. There was a machine in the kitchen which could extract the juice of two hundred oranges in half an hour if a little button was pressed two hundred times by a butler's thumb.

At least once a fortnight a corps of caterers came down with several hundred feet of canvas and
15 enough colored lights to make a Christmas tree of Gatsby's enormous garden. On buffet tables, garnished with glistening hors-d'oeuvre, spiced baked hams crowded against salads of harlequin designs and pastry pigs and turkeys bewitched to a dark gold. In the main hall a bar with a real brass rail was set up, and stocked with gins and liquors and with cordials so long forgotten that most of his female guests were too young to know one from another.

20 By seven o'clock the orchestra has arrived, no thin five-piece affair, but a whole pitful of oboes and trombones and saxophones and viols and cornets and piccolos, and low and high drums. The last swimmers have come in from the beach now and are dressing up-stairs; the cars from New York are parked five deep in the drive, and already the halls and salons and verandas are gaudy with primary colors, and hair bobbed in strange new ways, and shawls beyond the dreams of Castile. The bar is
25 in full swing, and floating rounds of cocktails permeate the garden outside, until the air is alive with chatter and laughter, and casual innuendo and introductions forgotten on the spot, and enthusiastic meetings between women who never knew each other's names.

The lights grow brighter as the earth lurches away from the sun, and now the orchestra is playing yellow cocktail music, and the opera of voices pitches a key higher. Laughter is easier minute by
30 minute, spilled with prodigality, tipped out at a cheerful word. The groups change more swiftly, swell with new arrivals, dissolve and form in the same breath; already there are wanderers, confident girls who weave here and there among the stouter and more stable, become for a sharp, joyous moment the centre of a group, and then, excited with triumph, glide on through the sea-change of faces and voices and colour under the constantly changing light.

Paper 1

Now read the first examination task and respond carefully.

This is testing your basic skills for AO1.

0 1 Read again the first part of the source from **lines 1 to 9**.

Answer **all** parts of this question.

Tick (✔) **one** box for each question.

Checklist for success
- Carefully read the lines of the text stated in the question.
- Check the options given in each multiple-choice question.
- Skim and scan the lines to identify the correct information.

0 1 . 1 Where can the narrator hear music?

From his garden ☐

From a passing car ☐

From his neighbour's house ☐ [1 mark]

0 1 . 2 At what time of day did the narrator see the guests diving and sunbathing?

In the afternoon ☐

In the early evening ☐

Past midnight ☐ [1 mark]

0 1 . 3 How many motor-boats does the narrator's neighbour have?

Three ☐

Two ☐

One ☐ [1 mark]

0 1 . 4 On which day did the servants work to clean up after Gatsby's parties?

Friday ☐

Wednesday ☐

Monday ☐ [1 mark]

Section A: Reading

This is testing your skills for AO2.

0 2 Look in detail at this extract from **lines 14 to 27** of the source.

> At least once a fortnight a corps of caterers came down with several hundred feet of canvas and
> 15 enough colored lights to make a Christmas tree of Gatsby's enormous garden. On buffet tables, garnished with glistening hors-d'oeuvre, spiced baked hams crowded against salads of harlequin designs and pastry pigs and turkeys bewitched to a dark gold. In the main hall a bar with a real brass rail was set up, and stocked with gins and liquors and with cordials so long forgotten that most of his female guests were too young to know one from another.
>
> 20 By seven o'clock the orchestra has arrived, no thin five-piece affair, but a whole pitful of oboes and trombones and saxophones and viols and cornets and piccolos, and low and high drums. The last swimmers have come in from the beach now and are dressing up-stairs; the cars from New York are parked five deep in the drive, and already the halls and salons and verandas are gaudy with primary colors, and hair bobbed in strange new ways, and shawls beyond the dreams of Castile. The bar is
> 25 in full swing, and floating rounds of cocktails permeate the garden outside, until the air is alive with chatter and laughter, and casual innuendo and introductions forgotten on the spot, and enthusiastic meetings between women who never knew each other's names.

How does the writer use language here to describe the neighbour's (Gatsby's) party?

You could include the writer's choice of:
- words and phrases
- language features and techniques
- sentence forms.

[8 marks]

Checklist for success
- Select no more than three features of language.
- Make sure you give an example of each one.
- Make a comment that explains its effect by deciding on what it makes you think of, feel or imagine.

Section A: Reading

This is also testing your skills for AO2.

0 3 You now need to think about the structure of the source as a whole.

This text is from the middle of a novel.

How has the writer structured the text to create an exciting atmosphere?

You could write about:
- how excitement increases throughout the source
- how the writer uses structure to create an effect
- the writer's use of any other structural features, such as changes in time, tense, mood or tone.

[8 marks]

Checklist for success
- Select no more than three features of structure.
- Give an example of each one or indicate where they are with a line reference.
- Make a comment that explains what the feature does to the text and the effect this has on you, the reader.

Section A: Reading

This question tests AO4.

It represents 20 of the 40 marks for Section A.

You will find it helpful to re-read the whole extract before you begin.

Question 4 will ask you to focus on a larger section of the source material – approximately half of the extract.

Carefully read the selected extract from *The Great Gatsby*.

> At least once a fortnight a corps of caterers came down with several hundred feet of canvas and
> 15 enough colored lights to make a Christmas tree of Gatsby's enormous garden. On buffet tables, garnished with glistening hors-d'oeuvre, spiced baked hams crowded against salads of harlequin designs and pastry pigs and turkeys bewitched to a dark gold. In the main hall a bar with a real brass rail was set up, and stocked with gins and liquors and with cordials so long forgotten that most of his female guests were too young to know one from another.
>
> 20 By seven o'clock the orchestra has arrived, no thin five-piece affair, but a whole pitful of oboes and trombones and saxophones and viols and cornets and piccolos, and low and high drums. The last swimmers have come in from the beach now and are dressing up-stairs; the cars from New York are parked five deep in the drive, and already the halls and salons and verandas are gaudy with primary colors, and hair bobbed in strange new ways, and shawls beyond the dreams of Castile. The bar is
> 25 in full swing, and floating rounds of cocktails permeate the garden outside, until the air is alive with chatter and laughter, and casual innuendo and introductions forgotten on the spot, and enthusiastic meetings between women who never knew each other's names.
>
> The lights grow brighter as the earth lurches away from the sun, and now the orchestra is playing yellow cocktail music, and the opera of voices pitches a key higher. Laughter is easier minute by
> 30 minute, spilled with prodigality, tipped out at a cheerful word. The groups change more swiftly, swell with new arrivals, dissolve and form in the same breath; already there are wanderers, confident girls who weave here and there among the stouter and more stable, become for a sharp, joyous moment the centre of a group, and then, excited with triumph, glide on through the sea-change of faces and voices and colour under the constantly changing light.

Paper 1

Now read your examination task for Question 4 and plan your answer carefully before writing it out. This is testing your skills for AO4.

| 0 | 4 | For this question, focus on the second part of the source, from **line 14 to the end**.

In this part of the source, the parties seem glamorous and excessive.

To what extent do you agree or disagree with this statement?

In your response, you could:
- consider your own impression of Gatsby's party
- comment on the methods the writer uses to present the party
- support your response with references to the text. **[20 marks]**

Checklist for success

- Use clear, supported statements to address 'your own impressions'.
- Make inferences to show your understanding; what is suggested or implied.
- Focus in and identify some of the writer's choices of language or structure (the writer's methods).
- Comment on the effect of those choices: what do we think of, feel or imagine as readers?

Paper 1: Section A

Section A: Reading

Section B: Writing

In this final section of your Paper 1 mock exam, you are going to complete Section B of the paper, testing AO5 and AO6 and representing 40 marks.

You are advised to spend 45 minutes on the exam task. You must write in full sentences.

You are reminded of the need to plan your answer.

You should leave enough time to check your work at the end.

Select and complete one of the tasks below.

0 5 You are going to enter a creative writing competition.

Either:
Write a description of a grand or beautiful place from your imagination. You may choose to use the picture provided for ideas.

Checklist for success
- Write a structured five-point plan.
- Remember to use topic sentences.
- Plan a selection of interesting language and structural features to include in the description.

Or:
Write a short story, or the opening of a story, about a time when a party or celebration went badly wrong.

(24 marks for content and organisation, 16 marks for technical accuracy)

[40 marks]

Checklist for success
- If you write a short story, ensure it has an effective opening, a complication, a climax and a resolution. Make sure these features are clearly paragraphed and linked.

Section B: Writing

Section B: Writing

Responses – Section A: Reading

0 1 Read again the first part of the source from **lines 1 to 9**.

Answer **all** parts of this question.

Tick (✔) **one** box for each question.

0 1 . 1 Where can the narrator hear music?

    From his garden ☐

    From a passing car ☐

    From his neighbour's house ☐ **[1 mark]**

0 1 . 2 At what time of day did the narrator see the guests diving and sunbathing?

    In the afternoon ☐

    In the early evening ☐

    Past midnight ☐ **[1 mark]**

0 1 . 3 How many motor-boats does the narrator's neighbour have?

    Three ☐

    Two ☐

    One ☐ **[1 mark]**

0 1 . 4 On which day did the servants work to clean up after Gatsby's parties?

    Friday ☐

    Wednesday ☐

    Monday ☐ **[1 mark]**

Sample Response:

01.1	From his neighbour's house	✔
01.2	In the afternoon	✔
01.3	Two	✔
01.4	Monday	✔

My checklist for success

When I answer this question, I need to remember to:

- ....
- ....
- ....

Responses – Section A: Reading

0 2 Look in detail at this extract from **lines 14 to 27** of the source.

How does the writer use language here to describe the neighbour's (Gatsby's) party?

You could include the writer's choice of:
- words and phrases
- language features and techniques
- sentence forms.

[8 marks]

Marking Grid:

AO2	
Level 4 Detailed, perceptive analysis 7–8 marks	Shows detailed and perceptive understanding of language: • Analyses the effects of language • Selects a judicious range of textual detail • Makes sophisticated and accurate use of subject terminology
Level 3 Clear, relevant explanation 5–6 marks	Shows clear understanding of language: • Explains clearly the effects of language • Selects a range of relevant detail • Makes clear and accurate use of subject terminology
Level 2 Some understanding and comment 3–4 marks	Shows some understanding of language: • Attempts to comment on the effect of language • Selects some appropriate textual detail • Makes some use of subject terminology
Level 1 Simple, limited comment 1–2 marks	Shows simple awareness of language features: • Offers simple comment on effect of language • Selects simple references or examples • Makes simple use of subject terminology, not always appropriately

Paper 1

Sample Response:

Gatsby's party is made to sound like a big celebration through the use of the metaphor: 'enough coloured lights to make a Christmas tree of Gatsby's garden'. This makes me imagine a place filled with fairy lights and sparkle.

The writer uses a list of all of the foods: 'spiced baked hams', 'salads of harlequin designs'. These sound very special and make the reader imagine a delicious feast.

The writer uses a lot of descriptive phrases such as, 'five deep', 'full swing', 'enthusiastic meetings'. These phrases make the reader imagine how lively the party is and the writer emphasises this by using personification to describe the air as being, 'alive with chatter and laughter'. All of these things give the reader an impression of how amazing Gatby's party must have been.

Colour key:
- Clear opening statement and language feature
- Relevant quotation
- Sensible comment on effect
- Another language feature
- Useful and relevant textual detail selected
- Another sensible comment thinking about the reader
- Specific and relevant examples given
- Comment on effect with further language feature identified and exemplified clearly

Commentary

This answer uses some sensible choices of subject terminology, which are not complex in any way. These useful terms then all have clear, accurate examples to accompany them.

The comments on effect – the ones that show the impact on the reader – are clear and appropriate. They are sensible and do not slip into content or comprehension, but keep the focus on how the writer may affect us through his choices.

My checklist for success

When I answer this question, I need to remember to:

- ....
- ....
- ....

Responses – Section A: Reading

0 3 You now need to think about the structure of the source as a whole.

This text is from the middle of a novel.

How has the writer structured the text to create an exciting atmosphere?

You could write about:
- how excitement increases throughout the source
- how the writer uses structure to create an effect
- the writer's use of any other structural features, such as changes in time, tense, mood or tone.

[8 marks]

Marking Grid:

AO2	
Level 4 Detailed, perceptive analysis 7–8 marks	Shows detailed and perceptive understanding of structural features: • Analyses the effects of structure • Selects a judicious range of examples • Makes sophisticated and accurate use of subject terminology
Level 3 Clear, relevant explanation 5–6 marks	Shows clear understanding of structural features: • Explains clearly the effects of structural features • Selects a range of relevant examples • Makes clear and accurate use of subject terminology
Level 2 Some understanding and comment 3–4 marks	Shows some understanding of structural features: • Attempts to comment on the effect of structural features • Selects some appropriate examples • Makes some use of subject terminology
Level 1 Simple, limited comment 1–2 marks	Shows simple awareness of structural features: • Offers simple comment on the effect of structural features • Selects simple references or examples • Makes simple use of subject terminology, not always appropriately

Paper 1

Sample Response:

The extract is structured as a first person narrative, 'my neighbour', 'I watched'. This perspective means the reader sees all of the preparations for the party and the party itself through the neighbour's eyes.

There are time references right the way through the extract, 'Every Friday', 'every Monday', 'On weekends', 'the summer nights'. It shows the reader that there is almost a set routine to the parties as the same things happen each time and are seen by the narrator. It also shows the reader that the party was not a one-off event but something that happened regularly each week.

In the first part of the extract the narrator uses past tense, 'his station wagon scampered', 'eight servants ...toiled' but then the tense changes to the present 'the air is alive with chatter'. This seems to make the reader feel like they are actually at the party and part of what is going on, almost experiencing it for themselves.

- Subject term relevant to structure
- Relevant supporting textual detail
- A sensible comment on the effect of this perspective
- Identifies a second aspect of structure
- A range of textual detail to support
- A sensible and clear explanation of the effect of time references
- Some more clear and accurate subject terminology relevant to the structure of the extract
- Again a range of relevant detail
- Sensible and clear explanation of effect

Commentary

This answer selects three sensible structural features to work with: narrative perspective, time and tense. They all have examples, which are clear, sensible and accurate without being lengthy.

The comments on effect show that the student is thinking carefully about what those features are doing to the text before they write the comment on effect, which is then very clear and sensible as a result.

My checklist for success

When I answer this question, I need to remember to:

-
-
-

Responses – Section A: Reading

0 4 For this question, focus on the second part of the source, from **line 14 to the end**.

In this part of the source, the parties seem glamorous and excessive.

To what extent do you agree or disagree with this statement?

In your response, you could:
- consider your own impression of Gatsby's party
- comment on the methods the writer uses to present the party
- support your response with references to the text.

[20 marks]

Marking Grid:

AO4	
Level 4 Perceptive, detailed evaluation 16–20 marks	Shows perceptive and detailed evaluation: • Critically and in detail evaluates the effects • Shows perceptive understanding of writer's methods • Selects a judicious range of textual references • Develops a convincing and perceptive response to the focus of the task
Level 3 Clear, relevant evaluation 11–15 marks	Shows clear and relevant evaluation: • Clearly evaluates the effects • Shows clear understanding of writer's methods • Selects a range of relevant textual references • Makes a clear and relevant response to the focus of the task
Level 2 Some evaluation 6–10 marks	Shows some attempts at evaluation: • Makes some evaluative comment(s) on effect • Shows some understanding of writer's methods • Selects some appropriate textual references • Makes some response to the focus of the task
Level 1 Simple, limited evaluation 1–5 marks	Shows simple, limited evaluation: • Makes simple, limited evaluative comment(s) on effect(s) • Shows limited understanding of writer's methods • Selects simple, limited textual reference(s) • Makes a simple, limited response to the focus of the statement

Paper 1

Sample Response:

I agree that the writer presents a very glamorous and wealthy scene in the extract. The food seems like a delicious banquet, 'buffet tables, glistening ….. dark gold.' This suggests that even the food sparkles like expensive jewels. The writer creates a semantic field of wealth by using adjectives such as 'glistening' and 'dark gold' to describe the food.

The guests at the party also seem to be very glamorous and fashionable, as they have their 'hair bobbed in strange new ways'. The writer uses noun phrases such as 'enthusiastic meetings' and 'confident girls' to describe the guests. This makes me imagine people who are always socialising and have money to spend on the latest fashions.

We know that Gatsby must be wealthy because of all of the extravagant things at his party. For example he hires 'a corps of caterers', 'a whole pitful of oboes and trombones and saxophones …' and he has an 'enormous garden' to hold the party in. This suggests he has a huge house with a lot of land and space and can afford to pay for these massive parties. The writer uses a metaphor, 'enough coloured lights to make a Christmas tree of Gatsby's enormous garden' to emphasise how light, bright and glamorous the garden is and how wealthy Gatsby must be to own it.

- Makes a clear statement with support and an inference to make a good clear start.
- Identifies a method and uses subject terminology, adding in relevant examples.
- Makes a second clear point and uses a good choice of quotation to support the point.
- Another method with examples
- A clear and sensible comment on effect
- A good range of relevant textual detail supports this point.
- This is followed with another sensible inference to show what is understood.
- Identifies another of the writer's methods and clearly explains the effect as well as linking back to the key words in the task.

Commentary

All of the ideas in this response are clear and relevant. There are some very apt quotations used as evidence for the points, and the inferences show understanding and add weight to the agreement with the statement in the question. The answer is clear and organised in the way it links in the writer's methods, with correct examples. Their comments on effect are sensible.

My checklist for success

When I answer this question, I need to remember to:

- ....
- ....
- ....

Responses – Section B: Writing

0 5 You are going to enter a creative writing competition.

Either:

Write a description of a grand or beautiful place from your imagination. You may choose to use the picture provided for ideas.

Or:

Write a short story, or the opening of a story, about a time when a party or celebration went badly wrong.

(24 marks for content and organisation,
16 marks for technical accuracy)

[40 marks]

Paper 1

Marking Grid: 24 marks available for content and organisation

AO5	Content	Organisation
Upper Level 4 Compelling, Convincing 22–24 marks	• Register is convincing and compelling for audience • Assuredly matched to purpose • Extensive and ambitious vocabulary with sustained crafting of linguistic devices	• Varied and inventive use of structural features • Writing is compelling, incorporating a range of convincing and complex ideas • Fluently linked paragraphs with seamlessly integrated discourse markers
Lower Level 4 Compelling, Convincing 19–21 marks	• Register is convincing and matched to audience • Convincingly matched to purpose • Extensive vocabulary with evidence of conscious crafting of linguistic devices	• Varied and effective use of structural features • Writing is highly engaging, with a range of developed complex ideas • Consistently coherent paragraphs with integrated discourse markers
Upper Level 3 Consistent, Clear 16–18 marks	• Register is consistently matched to audience • Consistently matched to purpose • Increasingly sophisticated vocabulary chosen for effect, range of successful linguistic devices	• Effective structural features • Engaging with a range of clear, connected ideas • Coherent paragraphs; integrated discourse markers
Lower Level 3 Consistent, Clear 13–15 marks	• Register is generally matched to audience • Generally matched to purpose • Vocabulary clearly chosen for effect; appropriate linguistic devices	• Usually effective structural features • Engaging with a range of connected ideas • Usually coherent paragraphs; a range of discourse markers
Upper Level 2 Some success 10–12 marks	• Sustained attempt to match register to audience • Sustained attempt to match purpose • Conscious use of vocabulary; some linguistic devices	• Some structural features • Variety of linked, relevant ideas • Some use of paragraphs and discourse markers

AO4	Content	Organisation
Lower Level 2 Some success 7–9 marks	• Attempts to match register to audience • Attempts to match purpose • Begins to vary vocabulary; some linguistic devices	• Attempts structural features • Some linked, relevant ideas • Attempts paragraphs with some markers
Upper Level 1 Simple, Limited 4–6 marks	• Simple awareness of register/audience • Simple awareness of purpose • Simple vocabulary and linguistic devices	• Evidence of simple structural features • One or two relevant ideas; simply linked • Random paragraph structure
Lower Level 1 Limited 1–3 marks	• Occasional sense of audience • Occasional sense of purpose • Simple vocabulary	• Limited or no evidence of structural features • One or two unlinked ideas • No paragraphs

Responses – Section B: Writing

Marking Grid: 16 marks available for technical accuracy

AO6	Skills Descriptors
Level 4 13–16 marks	• Sentence demarcation is consistently accurate • Wide range of punctuation used with accuracy • Uses wide range of sentence forms for effect • Uses Standard English consistently with secure control of structures • Accurate, ambitious spellings • Ambitious and extensive vocabulary
Level 3 9–12 marks	• Sentence demarcation is mostly secure and mostly accurate • Range of punctuation is used, mostly with success • Uses a variety of sentence forms for effect • Mostly uses Standard English appropriately with mostly controlled grammatical structures • Generally accurate spelling, including complex and irregular words • Increasingly sophisticated use of vocabulary
Level 2 5–8 marks	• Sentence demarcation is mostly secure and sometimes accurate • Some control of a range of punctuation • Attempts a variety of sentence forms • Some use of Standard English with some control of agreement • Some accurate spelling of more complex words • Varied use of vocabulary
Level 1 1–4 marks	• Occasional use of sentence demarcation • Some evidence of conscious punctuation • Simple range of sentence forms • Occasional use of Standard English with limited control of agreement • Accurate, basic spelling • Simple use of vocabulary

Paper 1

Sample Response 1: Descriptive task

Response	Commentary
It was a perfect day.	
The sun shone down on the beautiful, magical castle like a Disney fairytale come to life. The castle had red rooftops made up of tiny tiles and turrets looking neat and perfect against the sky.	The writing is already showing it is descriptive and the sentences are clearly punctuated.
The castle had cream-painted walls like vanilla ice cream, just perfect in the bright, crisp sunshine. The castle towered upwards like a wedding cake just waiting to be sliced and it brought joy and happiness to everyone who had the chance to see it.	There are a number of linguistic devices used here (i.e. similes) and the work is using paragraphs clearly.
The castle had a million tiny windows looking out onto the sparkling, glinting water – as calm as calm can be. Who could be behind them, I wondered? I could imagine grand duchesses from the past in velvet gowns, or bored princesses waiting to be rescued.	You can now see a sequence or structure to the description and it is still matching purpose by describing and not telling a story.
The water in the lake looked so inviting; at the front of the castle was a jumping off point that allowed you to dive in and take a swim.	There is a good variety of vocabulary and a more complex punctuation mark is used accurately.
Right the way around the castle there were lush, tropical trees making it feel cool and shady. There appeared to be little secret paths in the bushes and trees. You could imagine in the past the lords and ladies taking a stroll through there or children running and hiding.	There is an added idea here, which is linked and relevant, and more interesting vocabulary is used.
Behind the castle were big, tall mountains all covered in bushes and trees. They were like guards, keeping the castle hidden from the outside world.	Another interesting simile used. The writing is clear all the way through and in Standard English.
The castle remains a hideaway, a secret place in the forest now; perhaps for film stars or celebrities to escape the paparazzi and have some peace.	There are some accurate, complex spellings in the writing and a sense of a structure with the ending.

Commentary

This piece is organised very clearly into paragraphs and has a good sense of a structure. It describes all the way through, like an outside observer, and does not slip into telling a story at all. There are a number of good descriptive adjectives used and some linguistic features (similes) added for effect. There is a good range of vocabulary used right the way through. All of the sentences are clear and punctuated and there are some complex spellings too.

My checklist for success

When I answer this question, I need to remember to:

- ....
- ....
- ....

Responses – Section B: Writing

Sample Response 2: Narrative task

It was the big day. Alice, the little princess, was turning 6. "Perfect Parties" had been booked to organise everything as both Anna and her husband had been working full time recently. They'd picked everything from the glamorous website, the cake, the themed food and the entertainers and it had all been paid for in advance. Nothing was too much for the little princess. The morning had been mostly spent playing with all Alice's new toys but now as the afternoon drew on they needed to get Alice into her special new party dress and get ready to leave.

They arrived at the church hall early, wanting to make sure they were the first ones there and ensure everything was perfect. Alice was bouncing up and down like a jack rabbit. They walked inside and looked around. The room was empty. Deserted. Surprised, Anna looked at her phone but there was no message from the company she'd hired to run the party and they'd specifically said that they would text her if anything went wrong. A few minutes went by and the first children started arriving. A little nervous now she sent an email to the company asking if everything was OK. Acting like it was nothing she moved back over to the new arrivals and said she assumed they were just running a bit late.

The final stragglers arrived and now twenty children were catapulting themselves around the room, getting very restless. The parents staying with their kids stood off to one side talking amongst themselves and looking rather disappointed.

Anxiety started to creep in as she stood there checking her phone as minutes flew by. There was still no response from the company. She called the number she'd been given in case of emergencies. The line rang dead and she heard an automated voice telling her that the number she was calling did not exist.

Slowly realising what had happened, she began to tell the other parents what had happened and attempted to come up with a solution. None presented itself and eventually the police were called. Disappointed children began filing out of the hall but most disappointed of all was the birthday girl. She sat in the back of the car, an air of misery about her. The presents sat unopened in the boot, almost forgotten about. They took her out for birthday pizza instead but it was unlikely the event of the day would ever be forgotten.

- Sets up a believable plot and creates a sense of the characters.
- Organises the work into paragraphs and creates a sense of structure and time passing.
- Adds some linguistic features to add a sense of the atmosphere.
- Uses a variety of sentences to create the appropriate tone.
- Uses some interesting vocabulary.
- Uses some engaging details to keep the reader's interest.
- Sustains the plot and brings the story to a neat conclusion.

Commentary

This is a clear and well-organised narrative, which is well planned and thought through. In clear paragraphs, the story creates a believable plot, which is well controlled and sensible in the time. As a result it has an effective conclusion. There is some use of interesting vocabulary to create a sense of the characters and their feelings and sentence variety is used effectively. Work is accurate and shows complex spelling and is constructed in Standard English throughout.

My checklist for success

When I answer this question, I need to remember to:

- ....
- ....

Paper 2: Writers' viewpoints and perspectives

Paper 2 Overview

In *Paper 2 Writers' viewpoints and perspectives* there are two sections: **Section A Reading** and **Section B Writing**. Questions will be based on sources, which will be two linked texts.

The maximum marks for this paper are 80 marks and the time allowed is 1 hour 45 minutes. Before you begin writing, you are advised to spend about 15 minutes reading through the two sources and the five questions that you need to answer. You should also allow enough time at the end to read through / check your answers.

In Paper 2 Section A of the exam, you will be assessed on the quality of your **reading**. You will be asked to read two pieces of source material from non-fiction texts. One will be from the 19th century and the other will be more modern, from either the 20th or 21st century. You are unlikely to have seen the passages before.

Your job is to apply your skills of reading and analysis to answer the questions about the sources.

You are advised to spend about **1 hour** on this section. You need to read and complete four questions worth **40 marks** – half of the marks for the paper.

In Paper 2 Section B of the exam, you will be assessed on the quality of your **writing**. You will be asked to write an extended writing response presenting a viewpoint.

You are advised to spend about **45 minutes** on this section. You need to complete **one** question worth **40 marks** – half of the marks for the paper. You will be awarded up to 24 marks for content and organisation, and up to 16 marks for technical accuracy.

Section A: Reading

*Begin by carefully reading the extract below. It is taken from the **memoir** of Steve Backshall, an explorer and natural history TV presenter, written in 2011. In it, he describes a journey on a river with his film crew in Papua New Guinea.*

Source A

As if to prove the doubters right, that very afternoon I was running the boat out from a small creek on to the main river, and the engine stalled and stopped dead. As I frantically tried to restart it, yanking on the starter cord, our little boat got caught up in a furious whirlpool at the mouth of the creek, and all hell broke loose. It got spun round and round in dizzying circles, and on each turn the side was
5 dragged under water and brown river poured in. Pretty soon we were up to our knees.

I abandoned the engine and took up my paddle, frenziedly trying to pull us out of the maelstrom, as the folks in the other boat yelled and screamed at us from outside the whirlpool. Finally, the rapids spat us out and we were cast off downstream, dragged under a rocky overhang, then out into the rapids again. Relieved, I breathed out and flopped down in the boat, but the other boat was yelling
10 again: 'PADDLE, BLOODY PADDLE, STEVE!'.

I looked up, saw that we were passing the safety of a rocky bank, and just beyond it downstream was a fierce rapid that could spell danger. I struck for shore, and at the last moment jumped out into the flow and dragged the boat to safety.

The mood in the camp is quite sombre as we continue packing for our journey downstream. The
15 foreboding of the doubters has spread, and some of the crew honestly think they may never see us again. For a while the tension infects me too, and I find myself anticipating the worst.

Somewhat inevitably, we head off downriver prepared for a hell ride we might never return from. In the event, it turned into a fabulous cruise through one of the most beautiful prehistoric environments I'd ever seen. Maybe six miles downstream of basecamp was as far as anyone had ventured before,
20 so we immediately felt as if we were blazing a trail into the wilderness. The shallow forested slopes prevalent around basecamp soon disappeared, as the river plunged into a gorge with vertical limestone cliff faces a hundred metres high on both sides. Massive waterfalls plunged down into the river every hundred metres or so, creating vast clouds of spray billowing up into the sunlight.

Every one of the waterfalls is spectacular enough that if it were in Europe people would travel
25 hundreds of miles to see it. Here in the forests of New Guinea there are hundreds, sometimes four or five down one riverside in the space of a couple of hundred metres. It is one of the most awe-inspiring places, truly a wonder of the world. The promised terror-ride though, couldn't have been less in evidence. All our lifelines, lifejackets and secured equipment looked totally over the top as we roared through that paradise on our outboard-driven dinghies. I'd had scarier drives down to Tesco.

Paper 2

Now read your first examination task and respond carefully.

This is testing your basic comprehension skills for AO1.

0 1 Read again the first part of **Source A** from **lines 1 to 10**.

Choose **four** statements below that are **true**.

- Shade the circles in the boxes of the ones that you think are **true**.
- Choose a maximum of **four** statements.
- If you make an error, cross out the **whole box**.
- If you change your mind and require a statement that has been crossed out, then draw a circle around the box.

[4 marks]

A Steve stopped dead as he was sailing out of the creek.

B Steve Backshall took his boat out onto the main river.

C The boat was turning round fast in a whirlpool.

D Steve remained very calm as he tried to start the boat's engine.

E When Steve flopped down in the boat, he was out of danger at last.

F The river flooded the boat up to their knees.

G The people in the other boat had to drag Steve's boat to safety.

H Steve had to use a paddle to try to get out of the swirling water.

Checklist for success

- Skim and scan to locate the relevant information in the extract.
- Be aware that the wording of the statement may be different from the information in the extract.
- Use your skills of inference to decide if the statement is true or false.

Section A: Reading

This is also testing your skills for AO1.

Read the second piece of source material carefully (Source B). It is an essay taken from Travels in West Africa, a collection of writing by the Victorian female explorer Mary Kingsley and published in 1897. Here she writes about her journey down the Ogowé River in West Central Africa.

Source B

On we paddled a long way before we picked up village number one, mentioned in that chart. On again, still longer, till we came to village number two. Village number three hove in sight high up on a mountain side soon after, but it was getting dark and the water worse, and the hillsides growing higher and higher into nobly shaped mountains, forming, with their forest-graced steep sides, a ravine that, in
5   the gathering gloom, looked like an alley-way made of iron, for the foaming Ogowé. Village number four we anxiously looked for; village number four we never saw; for round us came the dark, seeming to come out on to the river from the forests and the side ravines, where for some hours we had seen it sleeping, like a sailor with his clothes on in bad weather. On we paddled, looking for signs of village fires, and seeing then not.

10   About 8pm we came to a corner, a bad one; but we were unable to leap on to the bank and haul around, not being able to see either the details or the exact position of the said bank, and we felt, I think naturally, disinclined to spring in the direction of bits of country as we had had experience of during the afternoon.

About 9.30 we got into a savage rapid. We fought it inch by inch. The canoe jammed herself on some
15   barely sunken rocks in it. We shoved her off over them. She tilted over and chucked us out. The rocks round being just awash, we survived and got her straight again, and got into her and drove her unmercifully; she struck again and bucked like a broncho, and we fell in heaps upon each other, but stayed inside that time. […] We sorted ourselves out hastily and sent her at it again. Smash went a sorely tried pole and paddle. Round and round we spun in an exultant whirlpool, which, in a light-
20   hearted, maliciously joking way, hurled us tail first out of it into the current.

Unpleasant as going through the rapids was, when circumstances took us into the black current we fared no better. For good all-round inconvenience, give me going full tilt in the dark into the branches of a fallen tree at the pace we were going then – and crash, swish, crackle and there you are, hung up with a bough pressing against your chest, and your hair being torn out and your clothes ribboned by
25   others, while the wicked river is trying to drag away the canoe from under you.

Our eyes, now trained to the darkness, observed pretty close to us a big lump of land, looming up out of the river This we subsequently found out was Kembe Island. The rocks and foam on either side stretched away into the darkness, and high above us against the star-lit sky stood out clearly the summits of the mountains of the Sierra del Cristal.

Paper 2

0 2 You need to refer to **Source A** and **Source B** for this question.

The writers in **Source A** and **Source B** are travelling by boat through different places.

What can you infer about the differences between the two places? [8 marks]

> ## Checklist for success
> - Make clear statements in your own words, addressing the question directly.
> - Support those statements with selected quotations.
> - Make inferences to show your understanding.
> - Remember this is an 8-mark short-answer task.

Paper 2: Section A 37

Section A: Reading

Paper 2

This is testing your skills for AO2 – identifying and commenting on the use of language in the text and its effect on you, the reader.

0 3 You now need to refer only to **Source B** from **lines 14 to 20** (below).

How does Mary Kingsley use language to make you, the reader, feel the danger and tension of her experience? **[12 marks]**

About 9.30 we got into a savage rapid. We fought it inch by inch. The canoe jammed herself on some
15 barely sunken rocks in it. We shoved her off over them. She tilted over and chucked us out. The rocks round being just awash, we survived and got her straight again, and got into her and drove her unmercifully; she struck again and bucked like a broncho, and we fell in heaps upon each other, but stayed inside that time. We sorted ourselves out hastily and sent her at it again. Smash went a sorely tried pole and paddle. Round and round we spun in an exultant whirlpool, which, in a light-
20 hearted, maliciously joking way, hurled us tail first out of it into the current.

Checklist for success

- In this response, select no more than three language features.
- Make sure you give an example of each one.
- Make a comment on effect by deciding what it makes you think of, feel or imagine.

Section A: Reading

Section A: Reading

This question is testing your skills for AO3 comparison.

It represents 16 of the 40 marks for Section A.

You will find it helpful to plan carefully for this task before you begin to write.

Question 4 will ask you to focus on the writers and their viewpoints in both pieces of source material and you may select your ideas from anywhere in the sources.

Carefully read your examination task for Question 4 and plan your answer using the bullet points to guide you.

0 4   For this question, you need to refer to the **whole of Source A** together with the **whole of Source B**.

Compare how the writers have conveyed their different feelings and perspectives about their experiences of exploring by boat.

In your answer, you could:
- compare their different feelings and perspectives
- comment on the methods the writers use to convey their feelings and perspectives
- support your response with references to both texts.

[16 marks]

Checklist for success

- Look for two key sections in each text that will help you answer the question clearly.
- Plan your response carefully so that you can write up your ideas more confidently and concisely.
- Write about what you can **infer** about each writer's feelings and perspectives using your AO1 skills.
- Write about the **methods** each writer uses to present those feelings and comment on how they make you feel as a reader using your AO2 skills.

Paper 2

Section A: Reading

Section B: Writing

In this final section of your Paper 2 mock exam, you are going to complete Section B of the paper, testing AO5 and AO6 and worth 40 marks. There will be one task to respond to.

Remember:
- you are advised to spend 45 minutes on the exam task
- you must write in full sentences
- you are reminded of the need to plan your answer
- you should leave enough time to check your work at the end.

0 5 'Many people think that you can only explore and have adventures in faraway places. They ignore what is exciting closer to home.'

Write an article for a magazine presenting your point of view on a place you know well.

(24 marks for content and organisation,
16 marks for technical accuracy)
[40 marks]

Checklist for success

A successful response should include:
- a clear sense of your point of view and your reasons for it
- a convincing argument, supported by well-developed ideas
- language style and rhetorical features matched to the task and audience
- a structure that is persuasive and logical.

Section B: Writing

Section B: Writing

Responses – Section A: Reading

0 1 Read again the first part of **Source A** from **lines 1 to 10**.

Choose **four** statements below that are **true**.

- Shade the circles in the boxes of the ones that you think are **true**.
- Choose a maximum of **four** statements.
- If you make an error, cross out the **whole box**.
- If you change your mind and require a statement that has been crossed out, then draw a circle around the box.

[4 marks]

- A Steve stopped dead as he was sailing out of the creek.
- B Steve Backshall took his boat out onto the main river.
- C The boat was turning round fast in a whirlpool.
- D Steve remained very calm as he tried to start the boat's engine.
- E When Steve flopped down in the boat, he was out of danger at last.
- F The river flooded the boat up to their knees.
- G The people in the other boat had to drag Steve's boat to safety.
- H Steve had to use a paddle to try to get out of the swirling water.

Sample Response:

B Steve Backshall took his boat out onto the main river.	●
C The boat was turning round fast in a whirlpool.	●
F The river flooded the boat up to their knees.	●
H Steve had to use a paddle to try to get out of the swirling water.	●

Commentary

The following statements are incorrect because:

- A It is the engine which stops dead, not Steve.
- D The text uses the word 'frantically' to describe Steve's attempt to restart the boat.
- E Steve is still in danger as he had failed to spot another approaching rapid 'that could spell danger'.
- G It is Steve himself who dragged the boat to safety.

My checklist for success

When I answer this question, I need to remember to:

- ....
- ....
- ....

Responses – Paper 2

Responses – Section A: Reading

0 2 You need to refer to **Source A** and **Source B** for this question.

The writers in **Source A** and **Source B** are travelling by boat through different places.

What can you infer about the differences between the two places? **[8 marks]**

Marking Grid:

AO1	
Level 4 Perceptive summary 7–8 marks	Shows clear synthesis and interpretation of both texts: • Makes perceptive inferences from both texts • Makes judicious references/use of textual detail to the focus of the question • Statements show perceptive differences between texts
Level 3 Clear, relevant summary 5–6 marks	Shows clear synthesis and interpretation of both texts: • Makes clear inferences from both texts • Selects clear quotations/textual details relevant to the focus of the task • Statements show clear differences between texts
Level 2 Some attempts at summary 3–4 marks	Shows some interpretation from one/both texts: • Attempts some inference(s) from one/both texts • Selects some appropriate quotations/textual detail from one/both texts • Statements show some differences between texts
Level 1 Simple, limited summary 1–2 marks	Shows simple awareness from one/both texts: • Offers paraphrase rather than inference • Makes simple reference/textual details from one/both texts • Statements show simple differences between texts

Paper 2

Sample Response:

In Source A Steve Backshall is in a place that is amazing to look at, 'a fabulous cruise through one of the most beautiful prehistoric environments I'd ever seen.' This suggests that the place was unspoilt and uninhabited.

However, in Source B, Mary Kingsley is travelling through places where people live, 'we picked up village number one.' This implies that the places she travelled through had signs of human life.

In Source A Steve Backshall travels through places which seem huge and impressive: 'vertical limestone cliffs' and 'massive waterfalls'. This suggests the landscape was spectacular to look at.

However, the place where Mary Kingsley is travelling seems more dangerous, especially in the dark; 'a big lump of land looming out of the river' and 'the wicked river' imply that the place is hostile for the travellers.

- A clear supported statement from the first source with a sensible inference.
- A statement of difference from Source B also supported and showing a straightforward inference.
- Selects more relevant textual detail from Source A and adds a second straightforward inference.
- Another clear and sensible statement of difference with support.

Commentary

The response makes two clear statements for each source and shows the difference between them. These are both supported with useful quotations from the texts.

There are clear inferences or suggestions made from both texts to show understanding of what is different about the two places.

My checklist for success

When I answer this question, I need to remember to:

- ....
- ....
- ....
- ....

Responses – Section A: Reading

0 3 You now need to refer only to **Source B** from **lines 14 to 20**.

How does Mary Kingsley use language to make you, the reader, feel the danger and tension of her experience? **[12 marks]**

Marking Grid:

AO2	
Level 4 Detailed, perceptive analysis 10–12 marks	Shows detailed and perceptive understanding of language: • Analyses the effects of language • Selects a judicious range of textual detail • Makes sophisticated and accurate use of subject terminology
Level 3 Clear, relevant explanation 7–9 marks	Shows clear understanding of language: • Explains clearly the effects of language • Selects a range of relevant detail • Makes clear and accurate use of subject terminology
Level 2 Some understanding and comment 4–6 marks	Shows some understanding of language: • Attempts to comment on the effect of language • Selects some appropriate textual detail • Makes some use of subject terminology, mainly appropriately
Level 1 Simple, limited comment 1–3 marks	Shows simple awareness of language: • Offers simple comments on the effects of language • Selects simple references or textual details • Makes simple use of subject terminology, not always appropriately

Paper 2

Sample Response:

Mary Kingsley uses informal language in the extract when she describes how the canoe 'chucked us out' when they hit the rapids. This interesting verb makes me feel the sense of danger that Mary is in on her travels.

She also uses a simile 'bucked like a broncho' to make the reader feel the speed and movement of the canoe through the rapids and realise how much danger they could be in.

The writer also uses onomatopoeia 'Smash went a sorely tried pole' to help us imagine the sounds of the chaotic and dangerous situation they are in.

- Focuses on what the writer is using to craft the piece.
- Identifies an aspect of language and gives an example with a correct subject term.
- Correctly identifies a second feature with an example and explains how the reader is impacted.
- Keeps the focus on the writer and the techniques they are using. The comment on effect stays clearly focused on the reader.

Commentary

Throughout the answer there is a range of sensible subject terminology, which is used accurately and supported with relevant examples. The comments on the effect of language on the reader have been clearly explained and are sensible.

My checklist for success

When I answer this question, I need to remember to:

- ....
- ....
- ....
- ....

Responses – Section A: Reading

0 4 For this question, you need to refer to the **whole of Source A** together with the **whole of Source B**.

Compare how the writers have conveyed their different feelings and perspectives about their experiences of exploring by boat.

In your answer, you could:
- compare their different feelings and perspectives
- comment on the methods the writers use to convey their feelings and perspectives
- support your response with references to both texts.

[16 marks]

Marking Grid:

AO3	
Level 4 Perceptive, detailed comparison 13–16 marks	• Compares feelings and perspectives in a perceptive way • Analyses how writers' methods are used • Selects a range of judicious textual detail from both texts • Shows a detailed understanding of the different feelings and perspectives in both texts
Level 3 Clear, relevant comparison 9–12 marks	• Compares feelings and perspectives in a clear and relevant way • Explains clearly how writers' methods are used • Selects relevant detail to support comparisons from both texts • Shows a clear understanding of the different feelings and perspectives in both texts
Level 2 Some comparison 5–8 marks	• Attempts to compare feelings and perspectives • Makes some comment on how writers' methods are used • Selects some appropriate textual detail from one or both texts • Identifies some different feelings and perspectives
Level 1 Simple, limited comparison 1–4 marks	• Makes simple cross reference of feelings and perspectives • Makes simple identification of writers' methods • Makes simple references/textual details from one or both texts • Shows simple awareness of feelings and/or perspectives

Paper 2

Sample Response:

Both texts describe explorers on a journey by boat. In Source A Steve Backshall seems to feel very scared at the start of the source when his engine stalls. He says, 'our little boat got caught up in a furious whirlpool at the mouth of the creek, and all hell broke loose.' This suggests that Steve's boat is in a lot of danger and he is in a panic at this point. He uses adverbs like 'frantically' and 'frenziedly' to describe how he is trying to get the boat started again to escape from the danger.

At the start of Source B, Mary Kingsley seems much more calm, but she seems to feel that the journey is far longer than she thought. Mary tells us, 'Village number four we anxiously looked for' which suggests she is starting to feel worried that they won't find the place they are heading to before it gets dark.

Mary uses repetition of the word 'dark', which makes us feel that she is worried that they won't be able to see where they are going for much longer, and she also uses the adverb 'anxiously' to help us to understand her feeling of worry.

Later on in Source A, Steve is much happier and calmer when he realises they are safe. He tells us that 'The promised terror-ride though, couldn't have been less in evidence.' This suggests that Steve and the team had been worried about the journey, but it was much better than they thought. He uses adjectives such as 'fabulous', 'awe-inspiring' and 'beautiful' to describe the scenery, which makes us think that Steve feels really amazed by what he sees.

Later in Source B though, things get worse for Mary and she seems to feel more panic when she says that 'About 9.30 we got into a savage rapid. We fought it inch by inch.' From this I can infer that Mary and the team were in real danger in the dark and must have been feeling very scared. She uses lots of violent sounding vocabulary, such as 'smash' and 'struck', but she also describes it as 'unpleasant'.

Annotations:
- A straightforward linking overview.
- Makes a clear supported comment on the feelings of the writer in Source A with a sensible inference.
- Notes a method the writer uses with correct examples.
- Makes a clear comparative statement to link Source B.
- Identifies a different method used by the writer of Source B and links to her feelings.
- Uses a second part of Source A to show the change in the writer's feelings. This is supported and also explains a different method the writer uses.
- Again, explores a later part of the text to show the contrast with Source A. Keeps the focus on the writer's feelings and and also comments on the methods she uses.

Commentary

There is a clear understanding of the different feelings each writer experiences, shown by the number of sensible supported statements. All statements are supported with relevant quotations. There are a number of inferences and suggestions made to show the texts are understood. These lead to several methods being identified with references to adverbs, repetition and adjectives. There are the beginnings of some clear explanations of the possible effects of these on the reader.

My checklist for success

When I answer this question, I need to remember to:

- ....
- ....
- ....
- ....

Responses – Paper 2   57

Responses – Section B: Writing

0 5 'Many people think that you can only explore and have adventures in faraway places. They ignore what is exciting closer to home.'

Write an article for a magazine presenting your point of view on a place you know well.

(24 marks for content and organisation,
16 marks for technical accuracy)

[40 marks]

Marking Grid: 24 marks available for content and organisation

AO5	Content	Organisation
Upper Level 4 Compelling, Convincing 22–24 marks	• Register is convincing and compelling for audience • Assuredly matched to purpose • Extensive and ambitious vocabulary with sustained crafting of linguistic devices	• Varied and inventive use of structural features • Writing is compelling, incorporating a range of convincing and complex ideas • Fluently linked paragraphs with seamlessly integrated discourse markers
Lower Level 4 Compelling, Convincing 19–21 marks	• Register is convincing and matched to audience • Convincingly matched to purpose • Extensive vocabulary with evidence of conscious crafting of linguistic devices	• Varied and effective use of structural features • Writing is highly engaging, with a range of developed complex ideas • Consistently coherent paragraphs with integrated discourse markers
Upper Level 3 Consistent, Clear 16–18 marks	• Register is consistently matched to audience • Consistently matched to purpose • Increasingly sophisticated vocabulary chosen for effect, range of successful linguistic devices	• Effective structural features • Engaging with a range of clear, connected ideas • Coherent paragraphs; integrated discourse markers
Lower Level 3 Consistent, Clear 13–15 marks	• Register is generally matched to audience • Generally matched to purpose • Vocabulary clearly chosen for effect; appropriate linguistic devices	• Usually effective structural features • Engaging with a range of connected ideas • Usually coherent paragraphs; a range of discourse markers
Upper Level 2 Some success 10–12 marks	• Sustained attempt to match register to audience • Sustained attempt to match purpose • Conscious use of vocabulary; some linguistic devices	• Some structural features • Variety of linked, relevant ideas • Some paragraphs and discourse markers
Lower Level 2 Some success 7–9 marks	• Attempts to match register to audience • Attempts to match purpose • Begins to vary vocabulary; some linguistic devices	• Attempts structural features • Some linked, relevant ideas • Attempts paragraphs with some markers

Paper 2

AO4	Content	Organisation
Upper Level 1 Simple, Limited 4–6 marks	• Simple awareness of register/audience • Simple awareness of purpose • Simple vocabulary and linguistic devices	• Evidence of simple structural features • One or two relevant ideas; simply linked • Random paragraph structure
Lower Level 1 Simple, Limited 1–3 marks	• Occasional sense of audience • Occasional sense of purpose • Simple vocabulary	• Limited or no evidence of structural features • One or two unlinked ideas • No paragraphs

Marking Grid: 16 marks available for technical accuracy

AO6	Skills Descriptors
Level 4 13–16 marks	• Sentence demarcation is consistently accurate • Wide range of punctuation used with accuracy • Uses wide range of sentence forms for effect • Uses Standard English consistently with secure control of structures • Accurate ambitious spellings • Ambitious and extensive vocabulary
Level 3 9–12 marks	• Sentence demarcation is mostly secure and mostly accurate • Range of punctuation is used, mostly with success • Uses a variety of sentence forms for effect • Mostly uses Standard English appropriately with mostly controlled grammatical structures • Generally accurate spelling, including complex and irregular words • Increasingly sophisticated use of vocabulary
Level 2 5–8 marks	• Sentence demarcation is mostly secure and sometimes accurate • Some control of a range of punctuation • Attempts a variety of sentence forms • Some use of Standard English with some control of agreement • Some accurate spelling of more complex words • Varied use of vocabulary
Level 1 1–4 marks	• Occasional use of sentence demarcation • Some evidence of conscious punctuation • Simple range of sentence forms • Occasional use of Standard English with limited control of agreement • Accurate basic spelling • Simple use of vocabulary

Responses – Section B: Writing

Sample Response:

An Adventure on your Doorstep

We all dream of faraway places with golden beaches and palm trees as an escape and to help us to get away from it all. However, it's just not always possible for everyone to be able to afford those kinds of trips or to be able to take time out from work and family to travel for months on end.

Have you ever thought that it can be just as much fun to appreciate what you have closer to home? Only a simple bus ride can take you into your nearest town or city where I'll bet there are many places you haven't even explored on your own doorstep. When was the last time you stepped inside that museum or art gallery that is free to enter and admired the treasures inside? Probably not since you were in primary school.

Even without leaving my city, there are two or three huge parks where I can get away from schoolwork and revision and be in nature with my dog for just a couple of hours to de-stress. The great thing about exploring close to home is that there are lots of countryside adventures that most of us can get to pretty quickly either by bus or local train. For just a couple of pounds, you could be out of town and breathing in some fresh country air – doesn't that sound tempting?

And don't forget the seaside. We sometimes forget that we live on a small island and by hopping on a train or taking the coach we can all be at the seaside in just a couple of hours and enjoy the ride as part of the adventure. Who doesn't love a day at the seaside with ice creams and fish and chips of course, maybe a white-knuckle ride at Blackpool Pleasure Beach or even just a picnic on the soft sand?

So, next time you dream of an adventure in a faraway place, get outdoors in your local woods or parks, or hop on the bus into town or the train to the countryside or the sea that's virtually on your own doorstep. An adventure is what you make it, not where you are.

- Adds a title to create the sense of an article.
- Makes an immediate connection with the reader and the focus of the task with a discourse marker (However,).
- Uses direct address and rhetorical questions to connect with the audience and this also helps to vary the sentence structure. Explores a clear idea linked to the task.
- Explores a second idea in a clear paragraph.
- Explores a third idea with some more varied sentences. Shows accurate use of a range of punctuation.
- Makes a clear conclusion that summarises the ideas of the article and ends with a neat reference back to the task.

Paper 2

Commentary

There is a clear attempt to write an article here and meet the purpose of the task. There are three clear ideas explored in appropriate paragraphs with a useful introduction and summarising conclusion.

The vocabulary is quite straightforward but there are some interesting touches, such as the references to the rides, the sand and the 'treasures' at the museum. There are also rhetorical questions, which help to engage the reader and create a connection with the person writing.

The sentence punctuation is accurate and we can see appropriate use of question marks, apostrophes and dashes. Sentences are varied in the way they are constructed and Standard English is used throughout.

My checklist for success

When I answer this question, I need to remember to:

-
-
-
-

Notes